LA CROSSE COUNTY LIBRARY

Drawing DRAGONS

Carter Hayn

New York

Published in 2013 by Windmill Books, LLC

Copyright © 2013 by Windmill Books, LLC

All rights reserved. No part of this book may be reproduced in any form without permission in writing from the publisher, except by a reviewer.

CREDITS:
Book Design: Nathalie Beullens-Maoui
Art by Planman, Ltd.

Photo Credits: Cover, p. 20 DM7/Shutterstock.com; p. 4 Christophe Testi/Shutterstock.com (pencil); p. 5 Obak/Shutterstock.com (paper), Paul Matthew Photography/Shutterstock.com (eraser), 2happy/Shutterstock.com (marker), Iv Nikolny/Shutterstock.com (pencils); p. 6 Alain Benainous/Gamma-Rapho/Getty Images; p. 8 Universal Images Group/Getty Images; p. 10 Popperfoto/Getty Images; p. 12 Tibor Bognar/Photononstop/Getty Images; p. 14 Eightfish/The Image Bank/Getty Images; p. 16 tratong/Shutterstock.com; p. 18 Greg Wood/AFP/Getty Images.

Cataloging-in-Publication Data

Hayn, Carter.
Drawing Dragons / by Carter Hayn.
 p. cm. — (Drawing monsters step-by-step)
Includes index.
ISBN 978-1-61533-689-0 (library binding) — ISBN 978-1-61533-698-2 (pbk.) —
ISBN 978-1-61533-699-9 (6-pack)
1. Drawing —Technique — Juvenile literature. 2. Dragons in art — Juvenile literature. I. Title.
NC825.D72 H39 2013
743.8'7—dc23

Manufactured in the United States of America

For more great fiction and nonfiction, go to www.windmillbooks.com.

CPSIA Compliance Information: Batch #BW13WM: For further information contact Windmill Books, New York, New York at 1-866-478-0556.

A Legendary Creature	4
Knights and Dragons	6
A Knight's Legend	8
Spirits, Away!	10
The Dragons on the Bridge	12
A Powerful Symbol	14
Dragons' Toes	16
The New Dragons	18
Dragons Today	20
Monster Fun Facts	22
Glossary	23
Read More	23
Index	24
Websites	24

A Legendary Creature

Almost all **cultures** have stories about dragons. Dragons are mythical creatures that often look like serpents or other kinds of reptiles. Most dragons have scales and claws. Some dragons have bat-like wings. Many have large teeth and horns. Some even breathe fire.

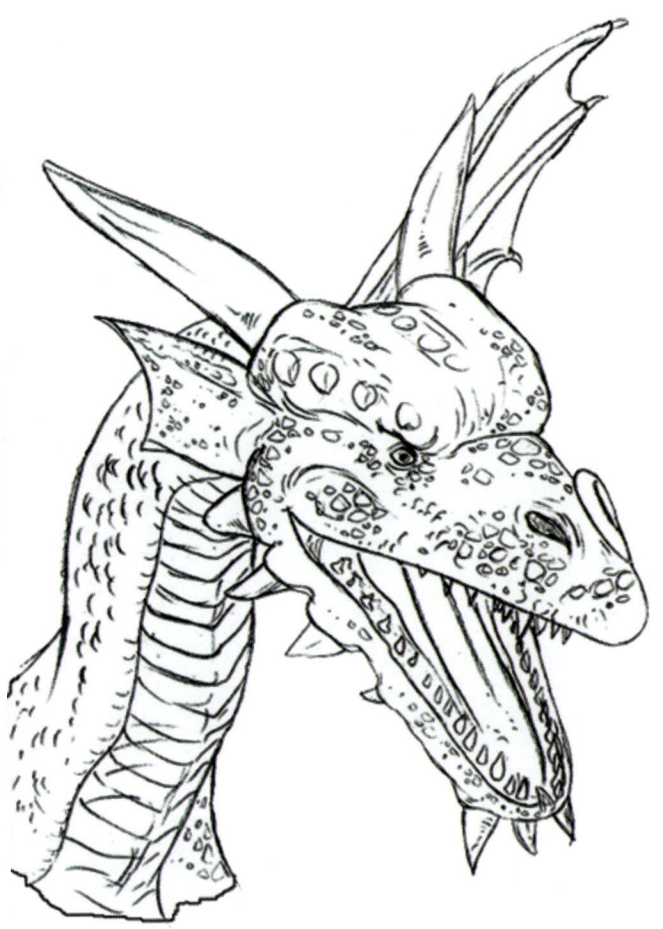

Stories about dragons have been told through the ages. In some stories, dragons bring good luck. In others, dragons are monsters that kill people. In these stories, a hero often slays the dragon and saves the town or a princess. In this book, you will learn about and draw both noble and monstrous dragons.

PENCIL

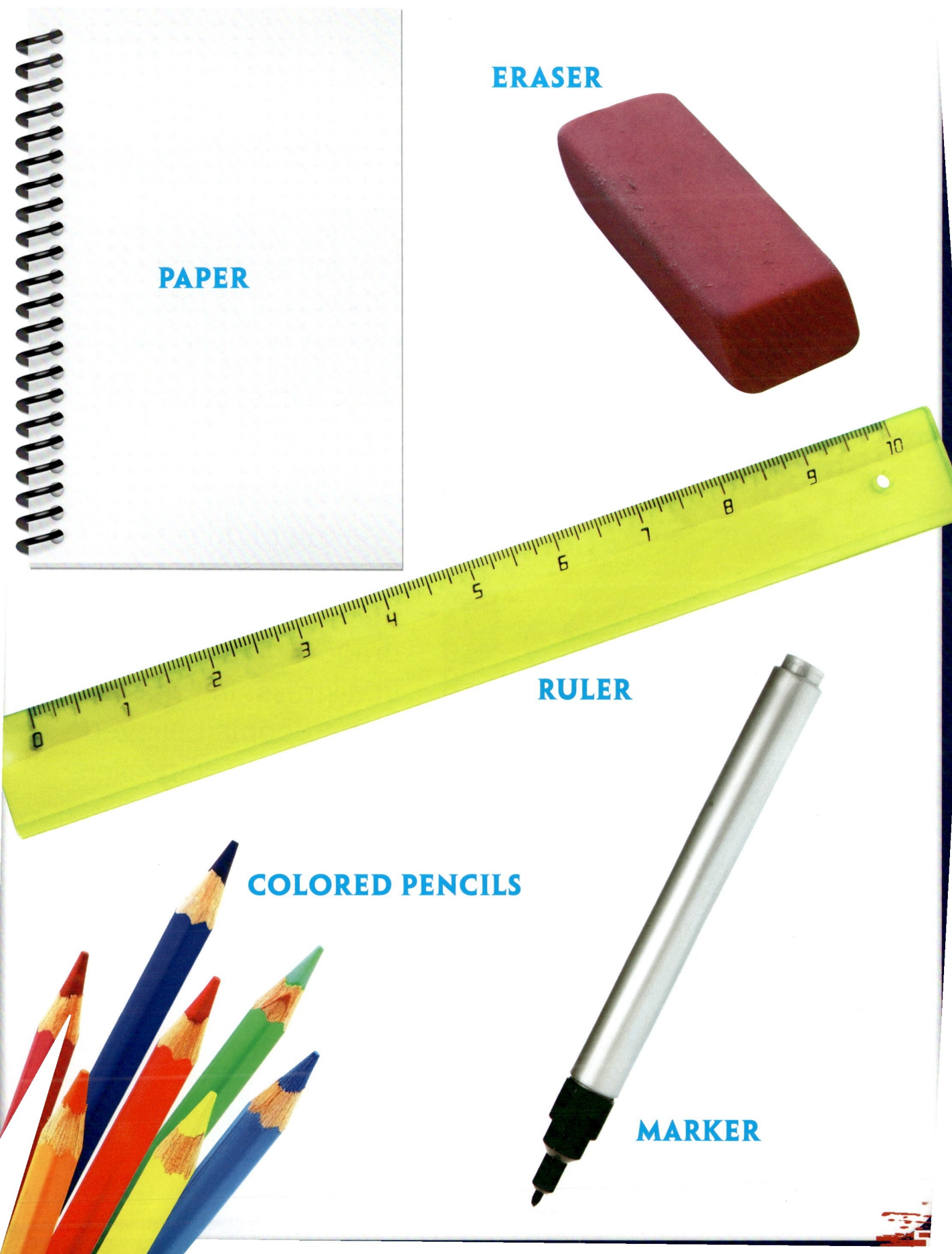

Knights and Dragons

In fairy tales, dragons often steal a **treasure**, such as jewels, or gold, or kidnap princesses. It is then a knight's duty to rescue the princess or recover the treasure by slaying the dragon.

In the Middle Ages, there were many stories about dragons and **damsels** in distress. In England some people believed that anyone who killed a dragon became a knight. Sometimes the reward for slaying a dragon was marrying the princess!

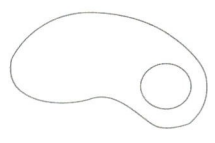

STEP 4
Draw teeth, claws, and spines. Add details to the hed and wings as shown. Draw the smoke and fire coming out of the mouth.

STEP 1
Draw the outlines of the head and the body as shown.

STEP 5
Add details to the wings and draw the scales on the body.

STEP 2
Add small ovals to be guides for the legs. Draw the ears, snout, and tail as shown.

STEP 6
Erase any extra lines. Color your drawing.

STEP 3
Add the wings. Use the ovals to draw the legs and feet.

A Knight's Legend

The story of St. George and the Dragon dates back to the Middle Ages. It tells of a dragon that terrorized a town in what is now Libya. Each day, one of the townspeople was **sacrificed** to the dragon.

One day, it was the princess's turn to be sacrificed. However, Saint George learned about the dragon and was determined to fight it. He killed the dragon, saving the princess and her town.

 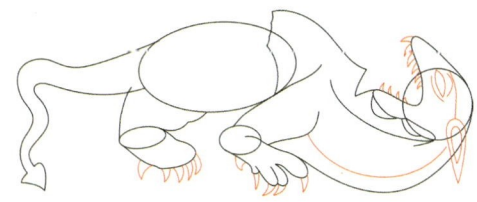

STEP 1
Draw shapes as shown. They will be guides for the head and body.

STEP 4
Draw the eyes, ears, teeth, and claws. Add a line on the neck.

 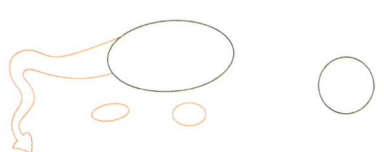

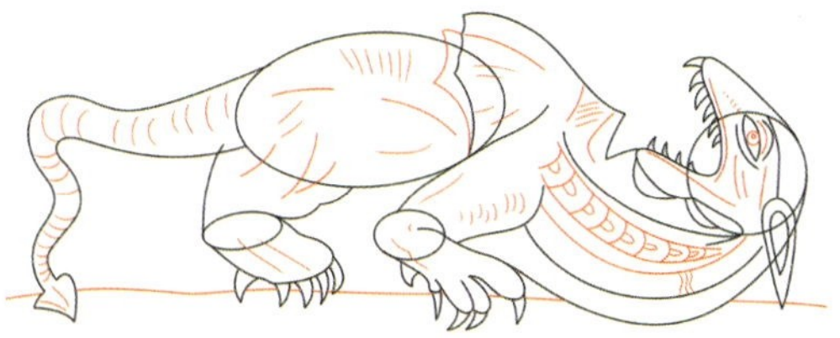

STEP 2
Draw small ovals under the body to act as guides. Draw the tail.

STEP 5
Add details to the head and body as shown.

 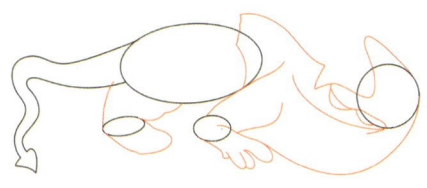

STEP 3
Use the guides to draw the legs and neck. Draw the wings and head.

STEP 6
Erase any extra lines. Add details to the face. Add color.

Spirits, Away!

Most Viking ships had a dragon head carved on their bow, so they were often called dragonships by the Vikings' enemies. Some people believe that the Vikings carved dragon heads on their ships to scare their enemies. In fact, the main reason was **superstition**.

The Vikings believed that having a dragon head on their ship would scare away bad spirits and sea monsters. These dragonheads were removed while the ship was docked so as not to scare away the good spirits that lived on the land.

STEP 1
Draw a round shape as a guide for the head.

STEP 2
Draw the ears, eyes, and mouth.

STEP 3
Add the tongue and draw the long neck as shown.

STEP 4
Add details to the ears, neck, and head.

STEP 5
Add more details to the face and neck. Draw some shadow on the tongue.

STEP 6
Erase all extra lines. Color your drawing.

The Dragons on the Bridge

Dragons are a popular symbol in Europe. The capital of Slovenia, Ljubljana, has a famous bridge called the Dragon Bridge. Four dragon statues sit on **pedestals** at the bridge's corners. Sixteen smaller dragons decorate the bridge.

Slovenian stories say that the hero Jason from Greek **mythology** founded Ljubijana. Legends say he killed a dragon there on his way home from his **quest** to find the Golden Fleece. He had won the fleece by putting the dragon that guarded it to sleep.

The Slovenians consider the dragon to be a figure of courage, power, and greatness. It is the symbol of their capital, Ljubljana.

STEP 1
Draw guides for the head and body as shown.

STEP 4
Draw the claws on the wings and toes. Draw the tongue, crest, and eye. Add details to the body. Draw the base.

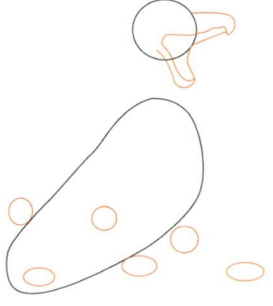

STEP 2
Draw round shapes as shown. These will help you draw the legs. Draw the dragon's snout.

STEP 5
Add the bone structure of the wings. Add details to the body, neck, head, and front legs.

STEP 6
After erasing the guide shapes, color your drawing.

STEP 3
Use the round shapes to draw the legs. Add lines for the neck. Draw the wings, toes, and ears.

A Powerful Symbol

Unlike European dragons, dragons from East Asia and Southeast Asia are respected and valued. They are often seen as powerful protective figures.

In Chinese mythology, the dragon is a symbol of power and good luck. The dragon is also one of the animals in the **Chinese zodiac**. People born in the year of the dragon are considered extremely lucky. Dragon dances are an important part of ceremonies and parades.

Most Asian dragons are water deities. They are connected to rainfall and bodies of water, such as lakes, rivers, and seas.

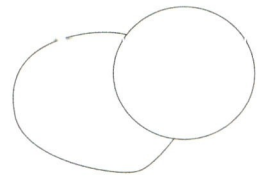

STEP 4
Add details to the head and horn. Draw spines under the mouth.

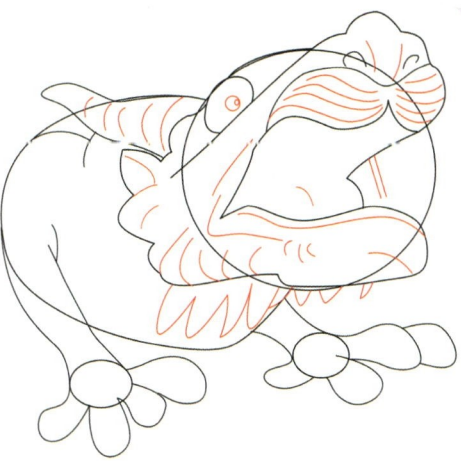

STEP 1
Draw shapes as shown. They will be guides for the head and body.

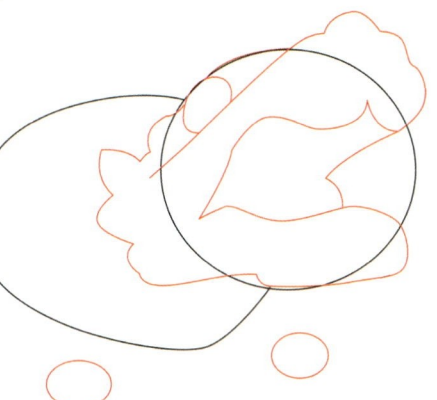

STEP 2
Draw the head as shown. Add two ovals to be guides for the legs.

STEP 5
Draw the scales on the back and body. Add the claws, tongue, and teeth.

STEP 6
Erase all extra lines. Color your drawing.

STEP 3
Use the ovals to draw the legs. Draw the horn, back, and nose.

Dragon Toes

In East and Southeast Asian mythology, the number of toes a dragon had was very important. A dragon with five toes was the Emperor's symbol. A dragon with four toes represented the nobility. A three-toed dragon was for lower-ranking officials and the general public.

Though the dragon is now used mainly for decoration, it is still considered wrong to damage an image of one in Chinese culture.

A dragon's color also has meaning. For example, gold dragons bring wealth, blue and green dragons represent the spirits of the spring, and white dragons stand for mourning and death.

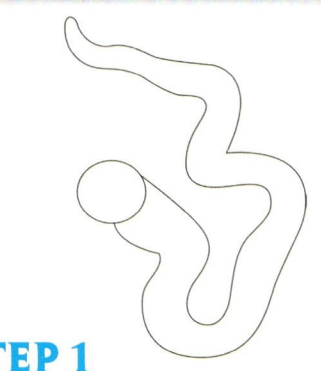

STEP 1
Begin your drawing with a round shape and a snake-like body.

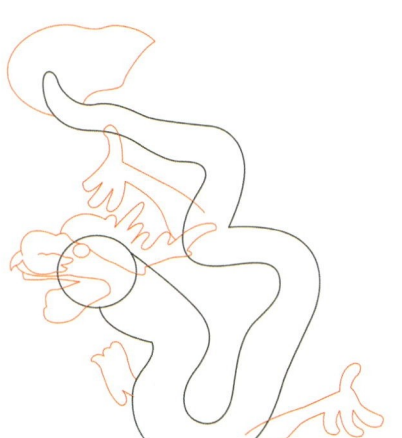

STEP 2
Draw the legs, face and end of the tail as shown.

STEP 3
Look carefully and add all the details shown here.

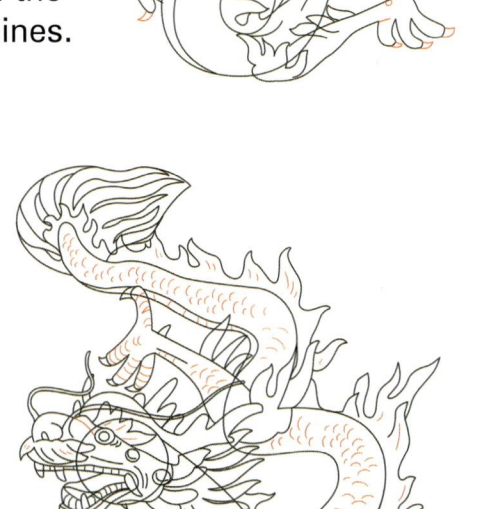

STEP 4
Draw the details on the face and top of the head. Erase extra lines.

STEP 5
Add scales and details to the body.

STEP 6
Erase extra lines. Color your drawing.

The New Dragons

Dragons continue to be present in popular culture. In 2010, a fantasy film called *How to Train Your Dragon*, based on a book by the same name, received many awards.

In 2012, a live show adapted from the film started its world tour. It has acrobats, projections, and 24 **animatronic** dragons, including the one shown above. It also has villagers and Vikings.

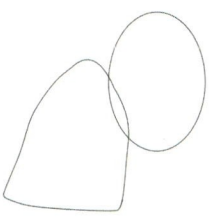

STEP 1
Draw two shapes as shown.

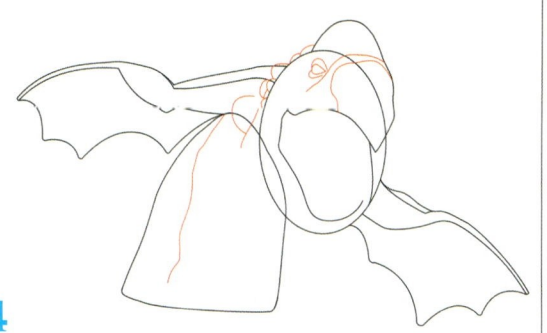

STEP 4
Draw the claws on the wings, the claw on the stomach, the tongue, and the teeth. Add the horns on the head and the lines on the nose.

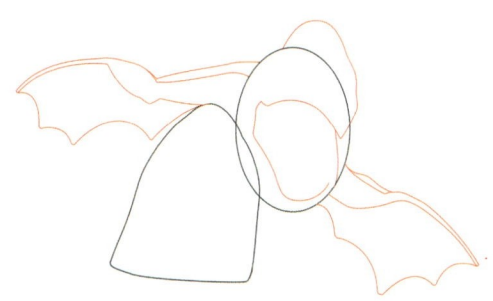

STEP 2
Add the wings and the shape of the mouth.

STEP 5
Draw the bone structure of the wings. Add details to the head and body as shown.

STEP 3
Draw the nose and eye as shown. Add bumps on the neck and the line along the body.

STEP 6
Erase any extra lines. Color your drawing.

Dragons Today

To this day, dragons are an important part of our fantasy world. From video games to role-playing, card, and board games, dragons are still very much present.

Dungeons and Dragons is one of the best-known role-playing games in the United States. Since its inception in the 1970s, around 20 million people have played the game.

Over the centuries, dragons have been represented as mysterious and magical creatures. Although they can sometimes be scary, their powers continue to fascinate.

STEP 1
Draw the guide for the head as shown.

STEP 4
Add detail to the neck, horns, wing, and head.

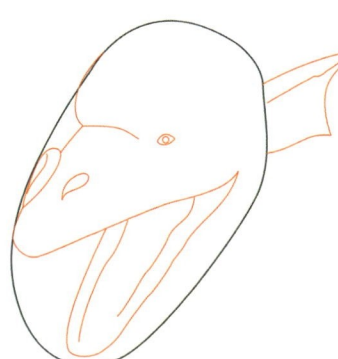

STEP 2
Draw the mouth and the snout as shown. Add the eye and left ear.

STEP 5
Add finer details and texture.

STEP 6
Erase guides, add finishing details, and color your drawing.

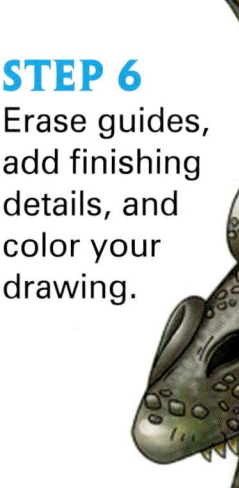

STEP 3
Now draw the right wing, horns, jaw, and neck.

Monster Fun Facts

- Killing a dragon is proof of bravery in many stories. Those who killed a dragon often keep the dragon's head and tail to show how brave they were.

- People once believed that if they took a bath in dragon blood, they could see into the future.

- While the dragons in some stories relied on fire to kill their vicitims, others killed with their poisonous breath.

- If you had an eye infection, people once thought that you should find a dragon, kill it, and use its fat as a cure.

- A sword dipped in dragon blood was said to inflict wounds that could never be healed.

- In some myths, when dragon teeth were buried in the ground, strong soldiers would be born from them.

Glossary

ANIMATRONIC (a-nuh-muh-TRON-ik) Having to do with puppets that are controlled by electronics.

CHINESE ZODIAC (CHY-neez ZOH-dee-ak) An old system from China that divides time into 12-year cycles.

CULTURES (KUL-churs) The beliefs, practices, and arts of groups of people.

DAMSELS (DAM-zuls) Young noblewomen.

MYTHOLOGY (mih-THAH-luh-jee) A body of stories that people make up to explain things that have happened.

NOBILITY (noh-BIH-luh-tee) Members of royalty or high-ranking positions.

PEDESTALS (PEH-duhs-tuls) Bases that help things stand upright.

SACRIFICED (SA-kruh-fysd) Given up.

SUPERSTITION (soo-pur-STIH-shun) A belief that something is unlucky.

TREASURE (TREH-zher) A thing of great worth or value.

Jeffrey, Gary. *Dragons*. New York: Gareth Stevens Publishing, 2011.

O'Connor, William. Dracopedia: *A Guide to Drawing the Dragons of the World*. Clovis, CA: Impact Publishing, 2009.

Roberts, Steven. *Dragons!* New York: PowerKids Press, 2012.

C
Chinese zodiac, 14
claws, 4

D
dragon blood, 22
dragon teeth, 22

G
Golden Fleece, 12

J
Jason, 12

L
Ljubljana, Slovenia, 12

M
Middle Ages, 6, 8
mythology, 12, 14, 16

P
princess(es), 4, 6, 8

S
sea monsters, 10
spirits, 10

V
Vikings, 10, 18

W
wings, 4

For Web resources related to the subject of this book, go to: **www.windmillbooks.com/weblinks** and select this book's title.